# The Dragons of Wellington

 Phyllis Bertin & Kaarina Bauerle

*Readers*

Pals
Fun in the Sun
Let's Go!
Camp Hilltop
Stand By Me
Are We There Yet?
**The Dragons of Wellington**

Copyright © 2021 by Intelexia USA, LLC.
All rights reserved. No portion of this book may be reproduced in any form without permission from the publisher, except as permitted by U.S. copyright law. For permissions contact: info@PAFprogram.com

**Authors:** Phyllis Bertin & Kaarina Bauerle
**Creative Director:** Elizabeth McGoldrick
**Illustrator:** Cathleen Daniels
ISBN 978-1-948832-29-8
**Printed:** July 2021
**Edition:** July 2021

pafprogram.com

# The Dragons of Wellington

Phyllis Bertin & Kaarina Bauerle

Illustrations by Cathleen Daniels
Creative Design by Elizabeth McGoldrick

Dear Reader,

    You are going to love this book! I am going to tell you an amazing story that happened a long time ago, long before you or I were born. You might think it is a fairy tale or a made-up story, or that some parts are far-fetched, but all of it really happened.

    When I was a baby, my mother would always tell me a bedtime story before I fell asleep. She would smother me with kisses, carefully tuck me into bed, and make sure I was cozy under the covers. Then she would begin.

    She had dozens of wonderful tales to tell, but I always chose the same one. It was a story that my grandmother used to tell my mother while she sat in front of the fire with her brothers and sisters. I loved hearing my mother's story over and over again. I never tired of it or asked for another story, because among all her tales, this one was the best. That is why I want to share it with you.

You will come across lots of wonderful things in this story—kings and queens, secrets and spells, and dragons. "Dragons?" you may ask. Yes, dragons. Real, live dragons! I adore dragons, don't you? If you ask me, dragons are nothing short of amazing. Before I tell you my story, let me share some facts you may not know.

Dragons are snake-like reptiles with legs. They come in all shapes and sizes. Some dragons are as big as a two-ton whale, while others are so tiny that they can fit in your hand. Some dragons have spikes that run along their backs, while others have none. Some dragons have bat-like wings so that they can soar high above the land. Others have wings, but oddly, are flightless.

A dragon's entire body is covered with hard scales to protect it from attack. The scales feel stiff and dry—like your fingernails. These scaly beasts also have long tails, sharp teeth, and some may even have horns! The horns of dragons are twisted and sharp.

All female dragons lay one egg at a time. The biggest females can lay eggs the size of a full-grown sheep. But most amazing of all is that dragons are fire-breathing beasts! Spraying flames is a wonderful way to defend yourself from an attacker.

At the time my story begins, dragons had become very rare. In fact, it was feared that they might become extinct. They were hunted because some humans felt that dragon scales would bring them good luck or keep them from becoming ill. The small number of dragons that were left had chosen to live deep in the forests.

The setting for my story is a lovely kingdom far away called Wellington. At least Wellington had been lovely until something very upsetting happened. Are you eager to hear more? Let me start at the beginning...

                        Edwin

# The Dragons of Wellington

# Welcome to Wellington

Many years ago, there lived a wise king named James the Good. King James ruled over the kingdom of Wellington. King James was called "the Good" because he was a fine ruler. He loved his subjects and his subjects loved and trusted him.

If you had visited Wellington back then, you would have been impressed. You would have seen hundreds of farms across the plains and hillsides. The farms were thriving, so there was always plenty to eat. Each week the farmers would load their wagons and drive into town to sell their crops.

What a delightful town it was! The second that you approached, you could sense that it was a cheerful spot. You would hear the laughter of happy children and chatter of friendly adults.

Dozens of shops lined the packed streets. The shopkeepers

included a blacksmith, a weaver, and a baker. Beside the river, there was a small mill where farmers would bring their wheat.

Streets in many other kingdoms were covered with trash and smelled disgusting. But the twisting streets of Wellington were clean and filled with delightful smells coming from the baker's oven. The homes were small but charming. Many had tiny gardens that were tended with care. Wellington was wonderful—better than any other kingdom.

King James did not live right in town. He lived in a massive stone castle high above the town with his wife, Queen Anna, and their son, Henry. Tall, thick stone walls enclosed the castle. It had taken many tons of stone and many years to complete.

It was said that over one hundred frightening reptiles swam in the deep ditch, called a moat, that ran along the stone walls. The moat and the tall walls protected the castle from intruders. It was quite a sight!

The castle was immense, with over one hundred rooms filled with many splendid things. The stone walls were covered with paintings and wall hangings stitched by hand. The thrones were handcarved and had rich fabrics draped over them. Anywhere you looked, there were lovely objects made by the finest artists.

Along the top of the highest walls was a wide walkway. The king's men could stand on the walkway and look for intruders. They could see the kingdom for hundreds of miles. King James would sometimes stand at the top of the wall and gaze at his kingdom—the town, the farms, the rivers, and the forests.

The sight of his beloved kingdom filled him with both pride and delight. King James was constantly thinking of ways to make sure his kingdom was well-cared for and well-protected.

One of the finest parts of Wellington was the town square. It was a plot of land where the children played, and their mothers and fathers gathered to discuss the latest gossip. The weekly farmers market was held in the square.

King James made sure the town square got extra care.

He ordered his gardeners to plant roses to make it look lovely and all kinds of trees to provide shade on hot summer days. He had scraps from his kitchen scattered in the square for any stray cats and dogs, so they would never go hungry.

The king sent his jester to amuse the children with clever jokes and silly tricks. Most Sundays the king's band would march to the square to play for them. Sometimes, both the king and queen themselves would visit and speak with their subjects.

There was nothing that the king wouldn't do for his subjects. Anyone who was ill would be sent to the town doctor. Anyone who was hungry could go to the castle kitchen for a hot meal. Anyone who needed a bed would be given a spot to sleep. Anything that was a problem would be fixed by the king.

Because they felt completely safe and content, the king's subjects rarely complained and were never angry. They felt that they lived in the best kingdom anywhere. There was nothing more they wanted. Life was wonderful in Wellington… until one day it wasn't wonderful anymore.

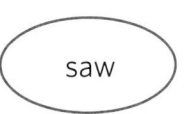

# An Amazing Sight

You must be wondering what happened to the town of Wellington. Let me explain. You see, the problems all started with the weaver's son, Cedric. The weaver had a successful shop that made and sold all the cloth in Wellington. Cedric spent many long days helping his father weave endless stacks of cloth.

It was a hard job for a child, but Cedric didn't mind. He was almost as tall as his father and just as strong. He never complained. Even when Cedric was hot and tired, he still had a smile on his face, as if he might start laughing at any moment.

The weaver's shop was open seven days a week, but Cedric had one day off to do as he pleased. And what he loved best was to spend the day riding his horse in the lovely forests of Wellington.

One day, Cedric was racing his horse in the forest when he felt hungry and stopped for a bite to eat. His mother had made him take some slices of cheese in case he got hungry.

While he was eating, he saw something fluttering wildly beneath the branches of a nearby spruce tree. He stared. There it was again! He was sure he saw a shadow behind the tree.

He approached the spruce tree as silently as he could. Carefully, he raised the bottom branches. What he saw was completely amazing! Extremely shocking! Really exciting! Under the spruce he saw a dragon—a baby dragon. Cedric was face-to-face with a real live dragon!

Cedric had been told many tales of dragons, but he had never seen one before. His father had said that dragons were wild monsters that breathed fire. But this tiny dragon looked pretty harmless.

The baby dragon was the size of a small dog, but she had a tail twice as long as her body and small wings. She was covered with shiny scales that shimmered in the sunlight. All of them were green except for a golden scale on the tip of her tail.

The tiny beast shrank back against the tree trunk. Cedric saw that the baby dragon was frightened and would not come near him. But in his mind, he saw himself striding into the center of town with a dragon by his side. That would be so exciting! He would be a hero! He sat down and began to munch on a slice of cheese while he was daydreaming.

The dragon lifted her nose and sniffed. Her nostrils flared, and she inched closer to Cedric. He smiled. He tossed a bit of cheese to her and stayed silent. The dragon stretched her neck and snatched it. Cedric placed another slice at his feet and the dragon came even closer.

While she was munching, Cedric carefully got a rope and placed it over her neck. After making sure the rope was not too tight, he got back on his horse. Slowly, he led the dragon to town, dropping bits of cheese for her as they went along.

As the pair entered town, some children saw the baby dragon and started to follow them.

None of them had ever seen a dragon before. By the time they all reached the town square there were dozens of excited children laughing and squealing with amazement.

The children started shoving one another to get a better look. The dragon looked more frightened than frightening. She hid her face under her tiny wings, shaking like a leaf. It was too much excitement for one small dragon.

Soon all the adults became aware that the weaver's son had come across a real live dragon. They gathered in the square to inspect it. Just like the children, the adults were excited and they all started hollering at Cedric at the same time. Where did he find the dragon? Did he steal her? Was the dragon wild or friendly?

The adults did not really know what to do with a dragon, but that did not stop them from giving Cedric advice. They told Cedric that most dragons needed someplace dark to live. They liked to eat hamsters and mice. Their scales had to be cleaned twice a month or they would become extremely slimy and smelly.

Then the adults began to bicker. Who would decide if Cedric could keep this beast? The town was in an uproar.

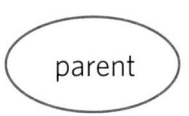

# A Gift Fit for a King

Meanwhile, back at the castle, King James was standing on top of the castle wall gazing at his kingdom, as was his habit. All at once, he noticed that something exciting seemed to be happening in the center of town. He wondered what was going on and decided to go see for himself.

Rather than walk into town, he decided to ride his prized horse, Cisco. On the way to get Cisco, he met Queen Anna and Prince Henry. "Where are you going?" the queen asked. She could tell at a glance that the king was excited.

"There is something odd going on in town. I am on my way," the king remarked. "Would you like to come along with me?"

Queen Anna said, "That would be lovely. I do not want to miss any of the excitement!"

"Is there a chance that I could come too, Father?" asked the prince.

King James glanced at his son. "You had better stay behind until your mother and I see what is going on. I want to be sure it is safe before you come."

The prince was saddened. His parents rarely let him leave the castle alone. The only time the prince rode into town or the nearby forest was with an adult. His parents said it was best that their son not go into town or play with other children. Rather, they felt he should spend his time studying and training, for someday he would be king.

His parents were not trying to be unkind. They felt it was their duty to make sure Henry became the most successful ruler Wellington had ever seen. But being confined within the castle walls felt like a punishment to the prince. Still, he always accepted his parents' commands.

He glanced up at the king. "Yes, Father," he said meekly. "I will wait here as you wish."

The king and queen got on their horses, raced out of the castle, and rode to the center of town. Once the king and queen appeared, a silence fell over the square. The adults stepped back, dragging their children with them. They opened a path so the king could see the dragon. He slowly approached the tiny beast and stopped in his tracks. You could hear a pin drop.

The king was struck speechless. He stared at the quivering dragon and then a smile stretched across his face. He grinned from ear-to-ear. He had instantly fallen in love with the baby dragon. "Where did you find this monster?" he asked with a laugh.

Cedric stepped up to King James and told his story. "Well, Your Highness, while I was taking a ride in the forest, I decided to stop for a snack. Suddenly…"

♛ ♛ ♛

When Cedric finished explaining what had happened, the king walked back to the queen to ask her advice. When they were finished talking, the king said, "This is my command. I adore this dragon. We must all comfort and protect her because she is a priceless gift for Wellington."

There was a roar of cheers and clapping. The king held

up his hand for silence and went on. "The first thing we should do is to decide on a fitting name. What should we call her?"

They all started thinking. "Wellington!" hollered one child. "Let's name her after the kingdom."

"Nice!" King James commented. "But you must admit it is rather long. That name would be longer than the dragon herself."

"Fido!" offered Cedric's father.

"That's a dog's name," Cedric whispered to him.

The king said, "We need something better. Not too fancy. Not too plain. Something ideal for such a priceless gift."

Then the queen spoke up. "Since you adore the dragon, why don't we call her Dora?"

"That's a splendid name!" remarked the king. "You are so clever, my dear. We will take Dora back to the castle where she can be well cared for."

And so it was that Dora the Dragon came to live in the castle. The king was delighted with his regal pet and treated her with tenderness. There was nothing he would not do for her.

He placed a fancy bed in front of the fireplace in his bedroom. When Dora was hungry, which seemed to be all the time, he had his kitchen staff prepare fine meals for her.

It seemed that Dora did not like eating hamsters and mice, as someone had said before. No matter how the rodents were prepared, she would not even lick the dishes. Rather, the fire-breathing beast had a taste for anything hot and spicy… and cheese.

Whenever King James had a chance, he would stroll from one end of town to the other with Dora. She was beloved by all. Wellington had its very own dragon.

# A Fateful Outing

One morning, King James bounced out of bed, eager for his daily outing. It was his habit to take a long morning ride with Cisco. He found that being outside made him feel peaceful.

The king loved the stillness and splendor of the forest in the morning. Since adopting Dora, he had taken the dragon along on his daily outing. He found that being outside was twice as nice with Dora prancing along beside him.

This morning, when the king glanced out the window, he found that clouds of fog were covering the town like a gray blanket. He could hardly spy the tops of the houses. No matter. Nothing short of a wild storm would keep him from taking his ride. He crept out of the bedroom without a sound. Dora, who had been crouching nearby, followed him.

When the king got to Cisco's stall, he found Prince Henry with his own horse, Glouster. The prince was carefully brushing his horse's mane. The king was proud of the way his son looked after Glouster. The prince always made sure the horse was clean and fed him twice a day.

The king greeted his son. "Good morning, Henry."

"Good morning, Father. Are you and Dora off for your morning ride? May I go along with you?"

The king said, "Maybe another time."

Prince Henry sighed. That was just what Prince Henry expected his father to say. "Well, be careful. It may be hard to see well in this fog."

"Do not fret, my boy," said the king as he mounted Cisco. "I have my trusty dragon. Dora would never let anything happen to me. Right, Dora?" Dora let out a snort and a puff of smoke, which made the king laugh.

As the king trotted off, the prince gave a final shout, "Please be careful, Father!"

The king rode to the castle's entrance, waving to the men standing outside the gatehouse. They all cheered when they saw their king with his trusty dragon by his side. Then he raced across the moat, around the town, and into the forest.

Dora had grown over the years and was nearly twice as big as when Cedric first found her. It was not hard for her to keep up with the king's pace anymore. Sometimes she trotted alongside Cisco. Other times, she raced in front of the horse, chasing the smell of small critters.

Dora loved exploring the forest. The forest was full of all kinds of sounds and smells that excited her. The king did not mind when she roamed around. He counted on her to come back when he called, and she always did.

This morning, Dora's ears pricked up as they approached a clearing. She stopped in her tracks. In the center of the clearing was a pair of deer feeding on fallen leaves. One of the deer was a massive stag with a full set of antlers.

Dora crouched low to the ground. She started creeping up on the deer, her snout twitching. Suddenly, she pounced.

It looked as if she was attacking them, but she only wanted to play. The deer bolted across the clearing and Dora raced after them until they were all out of sight.

King James cupped his hands around his mouth and shouted, "Dora! Come!" The dragon bounded back to the king's side. He gave Cisco a light kick to get going again. They rode deeper into the forest without noticing that the fog was becoming denser and darker.

The king had come to know the winding paths in the forest quite well. He had ridden along them hundreds, maybe thousands, of times. He smiled as they picked up speed.

Then, suddenly, as they galloped around a sharp bend, the king saw a mound of logs that had been carefully placed across the path. He shouted, "Jump," hoping Cisco would leap over the mound. The command came too late. The horse came to a standstill, but King James kept going, flying over the mound.

"Help!" the king shouted as he crashed, face-first, onto the ground. He lay next to the logs, out cold.

 thought

# Missing!

Some time later, King James was awakened by the sound of a horse trotting around the bend. When he opened his eyes, they were slow to focus. He saw Lord Vincent, one of Wellington's bravest men and a good friend of his. Vincent peered down at him. "I am so glad to see you, Your Highness. I thought something frightful had happened to you. How are you? What happened?"

King James sat up and glanced around. "I'm not sure. One moment I was on my horse, and the next moment I was seeing stars. I thought my eyes were playing tricks on me. I wonder how long I was out?"

"I do not know," said Lord Vincent.

The king was a mess. He was covered with mud and leaves. He ran his hand over his face to get the filth out of his eyes and winced. "Ouch!" he howled. There was a bump as big as an egg over one eye. The king asked, "What are you doing here?"

Lord Vincent explained, "Cisco came back to town without you. We found the horse roaming around the castle walls and we sounded the alarm. The entire town is out looking for you. Are you sure you are all right? You had quite a fall."

The king shrugged. "Except for this throbbing bump, I am all right."

Lord Vincent jumped down from his horse and helped the king to his feet. The king was still dazed and a bit dizzy. He fell against his friend. Vincent held the king until he got his balance. "Be careful, Your Highness. I do not want you to fall down again."

Vincent picked up the king's crown and wiped off as much mud as he could. Then he plucked a handful of twigs out of the king's hair and handed him the crown.

♛ ♛ ♛

Vincent led the king to his horse. "Now, Your Highness, you are still quite dazed. I cannot allow you to ride my horse by yourself. I will take you back to the castle." He mounted his horse and helped the king get up behind him. "Hold on to my belt," said Lord Vincent. "Try to relax. We are quite a distance from town. Do you think you have any broken bones?"

"No, I do not think so. I am just a bit sore. We should get started," the king said. "I want to get back to the castle and check on Dora as soon as I can."

"Dora?" Lord Vincent gasped.

"Yes, Dora," the king snapped. "I am eager to see her. I hope she did not get too frightened when I fell. Didn't Dora go back to the castle with Cisco?"

Vincent frowned. "Your Highness, I regret to inform you that Dora is not back at the castle. I do not know where she is. I thought she was here with you."

"WHAT?!" King James shouted, almost falling off the horse. "Dora would never leave me behind unless she were trying to find help. Something bad must have happened to her."

He began to panic. "Faster, Vincent. We must get back to the castle without delay! I will gather a hundred of our strongest and bravest men to find her. We will look for her all night if we have to."

"As you say, Your Highness," Lord Vincent agreed. He kicked his horse's side lightly so that she would trot faster. Still, their pace was too slow for the king.

The king could feel the bump over his eye throb with each step of the horse, but he was not focused on the pain. He sat in silence for the entire ride home, wishing that they would go faster. "Dora might be lost and all alone in the dark forest. She must be so frightened. I must find her at once!" The only thing he could think about was his beloved Dora.

# Down in the Dumps

Meanwhile, back at the castle there was a lot of chatter. What had happened? Where was the king? Queen Anna and Prince Henry paced along the top of the castle wall, hoping to see the king stride out of the forest safe and sound. They were scared something frightful might have happened to him.

Suddenly, Lord Vincent's horse appeared in the distance, with not one but two riders. The prince shouted, "Father! It's Father!" as he rushed down the steps.

Lord Vincent saw both the queen and prince approaching. He told them, "Our king has had a bad fall, but he is fine. It was by chance that I found him on the forest path. It looked as if someone had placed a mound of logs across the path."

"A thousand thanks to you, Lord Vincent," the queen said as she helped the king dismount from his horse and embraced him. Then she stepped back and inspected him from top to bottom. He was covered in muck and the bump over his eye was swelling. She hugged him again, even more tightly this time.

The king said, "I am all right now, but I am afraid that something bad has happened to our beloved Dora."

"Dora? Where is she, Father? I thought she was with you," said the prince.

The king said, "I am afraid she is not." His eyes welled up with tears. "We have no inkling where she might be."

Queen Anna did her best to comfort him. "Do not be distressed, my dear. Come, Henry. Let's get your father inside for a hot bath, and then we will decide what to do. We will track down Dora." They all walked into the castle and began to make plans.

The king was willing to do anything in his power to find the missing dragon. He offered 15,000 pounds to anyone who located her. He sent out a thousand of his best knights to the farthest corners of the kingdom hoping that someone had seen the dragon. But there was no trace of her. No one found Dora. Dora had vanished into thin air.

♛ ♛ ♛

Weeks passed. Still no Dora. The king became more and more unhappy. He blamed himself. He felt that he should have done more to keep Dora safe. He should have taken better care of her. He just sat by the window in his bedroom day and night staring at the entrance to the forest, hoping that Dora might suddenly appear.

The queen was becoming alarmed. She wanted the king to be his old self. She invited his friends to visit, but he would just stare at them and not talk. She had fancy meals prepared, but he hardly ate anything anymore. The king's jester, with all his silly pranks and jokes, failed to get even a smile out of him. Nothing helped.

Months passed. The king had not left the castle since the day he lost Dora. He stopped taking care of himself, and then he stopped taking care of his kingdom. The lovely kingdom of Wellington quickly went downhill.

Homes and shops were in dire need of repair. Gardens were overgrown and gates were broken. Flowers faded. Grass became dry and brown. In the center of town, no one was playing or chatting, and the farmers market was closed. The town square, once so full of life, sat silent.

Streets were filled with trash that made the air smell foul. Hungry strays prowled for scraps. Horses and wagons could not travel safely because no one repaired the roads. It was as if a dark and dreary cloud hung above the town.

Wellington was not the place it had once been. It had become a disgrace. There was talk about calling the kingdom "Rottington" and leaving it forever. Maybe life might be better somewhere else. King James the Good had become King James the Not So Good.

# Maid in the Kitchen

You might be wondering what Prince Henry was doing all this time while his father became more depressed, and the kingdom crumbled. Nothing much. The prince was unable to leave the castle even with an adult because his father was afraid something might happen to him, too.

Each day was exactly the same for Prince Henry. He spent his mornings with his teachers. There were many things that Henry had to know to prepare himself to be king someday, such as the dates of battles and the titles of all the nobles in the kingdom.

After lunch, he might visit the knights in the gatehouse and hear their tales of battles in faraway places. Sometimes they would invite him to play a round of cards to pass the time. However, they always let him win, so it got boring quickly. Sometimes he would play alone, pretending he was a noble knight dressed in shining armor.

Prince Henry did not have any armor of his own yet, but he liked to dress in fancy clothing and always wore his gold crown. He wore his crown when he ate, when he played, and even when he had his bath. He would have worn it to bed if he could find a way to keep it on. Prince Henry thought that if he did not have his crown on, no one would be able to tell that he was a noble and powerful prince.

Each day, the prince was able to go to the stable to see his horse and spend time brushing him. Glouster's coat shone like a knight's armor. However, being with the horse was not as exciting as riding him. The prince was bored and lonely.

One chilly day, Prince Henry was walking back from the stable when he passed the castle kitchen. He had walked by the kitchen many times but had never been inside. He thought it was not a proper place for a prince. However, on this day, the prince stopped in front of the kitchen. The heat from the ovens felt wonderful as it seeped out of the open door.

The prince could hear laughter and glanced inside. In the center of the room, a girl was chasing a little mouse around a table and laughing aloud. As soon as the cooks saw the prince, they stopped what they were doing and bowed. "Good day, Your Highness," they said.

The girl just kept laughing and chasing the mouse. Whether she did not see the prince or was just ignoring him, he could not say. When the mouse scampered across the floor and out the door, the girl came to a standstill. She and the prince stared at each other. No one made a sound.

♕ ♕ ♕

The girl had on a plain tunic that came down to her ankles and was covered by an apron. A small pouch dangled from her rope belt. All her clothing was covered with flour, as if someone had sprinkled it on her.

But what was most striking about the girl was her hair. She had lots of tangled hair that framed her round face and tumbled down her back. Her brown eyes twinkled as she smiled and broke the silence. "Good morning."

The prince frowned and said, "Call me Your Highness."

"Good morning, Your Highness," she said as she rolled her eyes.

The prince gave the girl a harsh look. "You forgot to bow. Didn't you notice my crown?" The gold crown was covered with sparkling stones.

She thought, "He thinks he is so high and mighty. Who could miss that fancy crown?" She bent deeply from her waist, so deeply that her hair brushed the ground. "Good morning, Your Highness," she repeated, struggling to stop herself from giggling. "Call me Molly."

"What are you doing in my father's kitchen, Molly? I did not think children were allowed inside."

"I spend most of my time here. My mother is one of the cooks and I help her."

"The next time you see me, remember who I am and do not forget to mind your manners." With that, the prince stormed out the kitchen door.

Molly had seen the prince around the castle before. He was hard to miss in his fancy outfits and crown, but

this was the first time she had spoken to him. "What a proud and snobbish boy," she thought. "He seems to care more about his title than being friendly. I wonder if he ever smiles."

The prince was thinking about Molly. Most other children were bashful, even a little fearful, when they were with him. Molly had just stared right at him. She almost seemed a little rude. There was something about Molly that was unlike any of the other children he had ever met. He struggled to put his finger on what exactly it was, but he kind of liked it.

# Friends in High Places

The next morning, Molly was in the middle of making some apple tarts when she glanced up and saw Prince Henry standing inside the kitchen doorway. She stopped what she was doing. "Good morning, Your Highness," she said, with a smile. The prince said nothing.

"Is something the matter?" asked Molly.

"You forgot to bow again," he said harshly.

Molly's smile faded. "Excuse me." Taking her time to wipe her hands on her apron, Molly bowed slowly and deeply, her hair in a jumble at her ankles.

The prince waited… and waited… for her to stand up. Feeling uneasy, he shuffled his feet. Still Molly stayed in a deep bow. He waited longer. He fiddled with his belt buckle. Finally he said, "Molly, please stop."

"Stop what?" asked Molly, as if she did not know what he wanted.

Henry rolled his eyes. "Stop bowing. Please stop bowing." Molly sprang up, with a smile so wide her dimples showed. Prince Henry decided to talk about something else. "It smells great in here. What are you cooking?"

Molly said, "We are preparing dinner. I'm making apple crumble tarts. When this batch comes out of the oven, I will save one for you to sample. People say I make the best apple tarts in Rottington—I mean, Wellington."

There was a moment of silence as the prince decided what to say next. He cleared his throat. "I was wondering, have you ever been to the top of the castle walls?"

The prince thought the top of the walls was a great place to go with Molly. At this time of the morning, chances were that the walkway would be empty. He thought that it would not be proper for a prince to be seen with a common kitchen maid.

Molly said, "I've never been anywhere in the castle except the kitchen."

"Would you like to see what the town looks like from the top of the walls? You will not be frightened of being up so high, will you?"

Molly chuckled. "Frightened? I won't be frightened. I love excitement. Going someplace I have never been before sounds great to me."

Molly looked at her mother who was scrubbing a kettle. "Mama," Molly said. "We are going for a walk. I'll be back soon to finish the apple tarts." Molly's mother was so startled her mouth fell open. She was speechless to see Molly going off with the prince.

The two children walked to the nearest tower and hiked up its steep, winding staircase. Now that he was alone with Molly on the walkway, the prince was not sure exactly what they were going to do up there. Meanwhile, Molly did not wait for the prince to make up his mind about what to do. She began dangling her arms over the side of the wall and shouting to the people far below.

Molly looked up at the prince and said, "Let's have a race." She began sprinting along the walkway with her hair streaming behind her. The prince quickly raced after her. They ran around and around until they were both worn out and flopped down on the ground. Molly laughed aloud, but the prince did not.

Nobody could say who had won the race, but it did not matter. Molly was thrilled to be out of the kitchen. Prince Henry was pleased to have someone to spend time with and to talk to.

While they were resting, Molly decided to see if she could make the prince laugh aloud. She asked him some simple riddles. No one had ever asked the prince riddles and they puzzled him. But they did not make him laugh or even giggle. He did not find them even a little bit funny.

Molly kept trying. At last, one riddle made Prince Henry smile. It was just a little smile, but Molly thought it was a good beginning.

Suddenly they could hear someone or something screeching in the distance. They glanced at each other, puzzled. Then they jumped to their feet and ran to see what was happening. They saw a small eagle on the walkway thrashing wildly from side to side. The eagle was trembling with fright and pain.

As the prince approached the eagle, it grabbed his ankle with its sharp talons. Now it was the prince who screamed as he struggled to get free. He howled in pain. The louder he screamed, the tighter the eagle's grip became. "Help!"

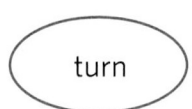

PAF
Level 170

# Hocus Pocus

Prince Henry struggled to escape from the eagle's grasp. The animal was not full grown, but its talons were powerful and sharp. Henry did not want to injure the little eagle, but he could not hold out much longer. Tears of pain trickled down his cheeks. "Please help me, Molly," he gasped.

Molly did not hesitate. She started walking to the prince and eagle, whispering softly. It was difficult for the prince to hear exactly what Molly was saying, but the eagle seemed to hear her whispering and fixed its yellow eyes on her. Molly stepped closer, and closer. Henry stayed completely still.

As she got to the eagle, Molly reached into the pouch on her belt and yanked out a chain with two sparkling gold charms. Molly bent down next to the eagle, dangling the chain in front of its face. Back and forth, back and forth, she swung the chain.

Her eyes never left the eagle's and her whispering never stopped. Little by little, the eagle settled down and fell into a trance. Its grip on the prince's ankle relaxed until the prince was able to free himself.

Now that the eagle was still, Molly could inspect it more closely. She found a deep cut on its wing. Grabbing a tiny bottle from her pouch, she jiggled a bit of yellow powder into her hand.

"What is that?" asked the prince. Molly said nothing. She was completely focused on her task.

She sprinkled some of the powder on the gash. At once, the powder began to bubble and sizzle. Prince Henry was flabbergasted. "What are you doing to that eagle? Stop it right now! I command you!" Still Molly said nothing, and the eagle remained in a trance, unaware of all the excitement.

Just as suddenly as it had started, the bubbling and sizzling stopped. Molly clapped twice and said, "Awaken!" and the eagle came out of the trance. It softly nuzzled Molly's face as if it were trying to thank her. And then the eagle opened its wings and rose into the clouds.

Molly's treatment was a complete success. Now that Prince Henry saw that the animal had been cured and not injured by her powder, he relaxed. "That was fantastic! Do you have secret powers? Are you a witch?"

Molly laughed. "Be careful or I might turn you into a frog!" The prince smiled. Only later did he remember that Molly had not really said whether or not she was a witch.

♛ ♛ ♛

From then on, the prince and Molly always spent time together after he was done studying and her chores were done. Sometimes they went to the castle keep. The doors to the Great Hall were kept locked so they had to peek into the ground floor windows.

Molly thought the Great Hall was extremely impressive. She was dazzled by its immense size and splendor. It contained a long table with dozens of chairs. At the far end of the room, two thrones rested on a platform. Behind the thrones was a magnificent painting of Henry and his parents. What Molly liked best was the fireplace, which was bordered with lovely carvings of forest animals.

Sometimes the children went to the stable to visit the horses in their stalls. The horses would greet the children by tossing their manes and stretching their necks over the stall doors. Then they would nibble apples right from the children's hands!

The prince had to admit that life was not boring since he had met Molly. And Molly was grateful that the prince allowed her to visit parts of the castle she had never been able to explore before. Over time, they got to know each other better. More than that, they both were growing to like each other. Henry, the Prince of Wellington, and Molly, the kitchen girl, were becoming friends.

# The Queen's Visitor

Life remained the same in Wellington. (Or should I say Rottington?) The town was in bad shape—filthy, smelly, and uncared for. The people were gloomy and hungry. They could hardly remember how excellent the town had been before Dora vanished.

They were beginning to give up hope. What would happen to their kingdom if the king's mood did not get better soon? What would happen to their family and friends? It was hard to stay positive.

The king remained alone in his bedroom staring, out the window. He waited for someone to tell him that Dora had been found, but there was no trace of her anywhere. It was as if Dora had vanished into thin air.

One afternoon, a peddler drove into town on a wobbly wagon lugged by a sad-looking mule. The mule looked as if it had not been fed a proper meal in days. The peddler wore a loose tunic, belted at the waist, and mud-covered boots. He had a silver loop in one ear, and a tiny tattoo of a crescent moon on the side of his face.

His mood seemed dark and unfriendly. Now and then, he would crack a whip over the mule, as if he thought it needed to be woken up. The animal kept plodding along, too sad or too weak to notice.

The wagon had all sorts of things dangling from its sides—brooms and kettles, ladles and spoons. The jingle of these dangling utensils made such a racket as it bounced over the loose cobblestones that people turned to stare. The unfriendly man just glared back at them and said nothing. They wondered who the peddler was and what he was doing in town. No one could remember having ever seen him before.

The peddler's wagon approached the castle and came to a standstill at the entrance to the gatehouse. "Stop!" shouted a knight who had been snoozing. "Who goes there? Announce yourself."

"I am Silvester, a humble citizen of Wellington."

The knight asked, "And where do you think you are going? This entrance is not for people like you."

"I have something important for Her Majesty, the queen," Silvester snarled.

The knight chuckled. "Fool! Do you think you are so important that I would take you to our noble queen? Give me the gift, and I will take it to her later."

"No," said Silvester. "I have to deliver it to her myself."

"Well, I will not allow you to enter. Give it to me, and get out of here, or you will face harsh punishment."

Silvester did not seem frightened by the knight. He picked up a small pouch in his lap. "Deliver this to Her Majesty. It will give her a hint as to why I am here. I know the queen will be angry if she doesn't get this."

The knight hesitated. He did not want to anger the queen. "Give that to me," he demanded as he reached up and grabbed the pouch from the peddler's hand. "Remain here. There had better be something fantastic in this pouch. If I bother the queen for no reason, you will pay the price."

"Don't fret. She will love it," said Silvester.

As the knight stepped into the inner yard of the castle, he saw the queen and prince coming out of the stable together. He waited until the queen was close and bowed deeply.

"Rise. You may speak," said Queen Anna.

"Your Majesty, there is a peddler outside the castle who insists he has something important for you. He says this pouch contains a hint as to what it is."

Queen Anna looked puzzled. "Something important for me? From a peddler?"

The knight said, "Yes, but he is a gruff fellow. I wouldn't be shocked if the pouch contains something disgusting."

"Be careful, Mother!" said Henry, as the knight handed her the pouch. "There might be something harmful inside." The queen nodded.

She loosened the cord looped around the pouch, turned it over, and jiggled it. Something fell out. "Oh, my goodness!" she said. She was flabbergasted! Right in the middle of her hand was the single green scale of a dragon!

# Bamboozled!

Queen Anna and Prince Henry stared at the dragon scale in amazement. "This is fantastic!" she said. "Bring the peddler to me in the Great Hall at once." The knight bowed and dashed off.

The queen and prince walked together to the Great Hall. Henry asked, "Do you think it is possible, Mother? It seems unlikely that a peddler has found Dora, and yet I cannot help feeling hopeful."

The queen agreed. "It seems strange to me, too. Still, I also hope this man has found Dora." Just then, there was a loud rap on the door. "Enter!" said the queen. The knight entered the room with Silvester.

"Your Majesty," announced the knight. "This is Silvester, the peddler I told you about."

He turned to Silvester. "Take off your hat and bow to our queen," he ordered.

"You may leave us alone now," said the queen. "Thank you for bringing this gentleman to me." She did not think Silvester really looked like a gentleman. He was strange, maybe even a little scary, but she was trying to be polite. "What gift do you have for me? Have you found Dora?" she asked.

"Dora? Who is Dora?"

The queen sighed. He had not found their dragon. She thought, "Green is such a common color for a dragon. I should have noticed that the scale is not the same shade of green as Dora's scales. It was foolish of me to think this stranger might have found Dora."

She was puzzled. She asked, "Where did you get this scale?"

Silvester explained, "Recently, I found a little dragon roaming around at night. I was afraid she might be lost, so I scooped her up and put her in my wagon and went home. I decided to bring her to you because the king has been in a gloomy mood ever since his dragon ran away. I'm offering to sell her to you."

"SELL? You want to sell a dragon to me?" scoffed Anna.

"Let's call it a fair exchange. I think your crown would do quite nicely in exchange for my dragon."

Anna was in a rage. "That dragon could help the king and possibly the entire kingdom. How dare you ask me for my crown! I am your ruler, and you are my subject. I could command you to give me the dragon."

Silvester said, "You can command me to tell you where the dragon is. You can try to force me. Lock me in a prison cell, but I still won't tell you."

♛ ♛ ♛

The queen considered what Silvester had told her. Maybe, in time, she could force him to reveal where he was keeping the dragon, but she did not want to wait.

She gently put her hand on her crown. She hated to part with it, but the king and the kingdom's well-being were more important than a crown, which could be replaced.

"All right, it is a deal. Bring me the dragon and I will give you my crown."

Silvester grumbled, "How do I know you won't change your mind?"

"I will not change my mind," the queen vowed.

Silvester wondered if he could trust that the queen would give him the crown. But he wanted it more than anything he had ever seen. He dashed out of the room and quickly returned dragging a small dragon by a rope.

The queen was astonished! The dragon had been right outside the entire time. She had been bamboozled! "What a fool I have been. I could have just taken her without giving him my crown. But a deal is a deal. I said I would give this swindler my crown, so I must do it."

Silvester handed the rope to Queen Anna. "Your crown," he reminded her. She started to pass him her crown, but he snatched it and was gone, without so much as a "thank you."

The queen and prince stared down at the dragon and smiled. The first thing she did was take the rope off the dragon's throat. It was difficult because it was so tight. "No need for that," she said, dropping the filthy rope on the floor and brushing her hands off. "Let us go upstairs. There is someone I want you to meet."

# A Real Gem

King James was sitting by the window, snoozing. The sound of the door opening woke him. "Has someone found Dora?" he asked hopefully.

"I'm afraid not, my dear," said the queen. "But we have something for you that we think will make you happy."

The king turned to look at them. He gasped when he saw the dragon. As he approached, the dragon started thumping her tail against the floor. He crouched down to get a better look at the little beast and she jumped into his arms.

The king got up and hugged his wife and son. "Thank you," he whispered. "She is magnificent—a real gem." He was delighted. "I will take this dragon for a walk so that everyone can see and admire her. I will introduce her to every citizen of Wellington. I will shout her name from the rooftops!"

He started to leave the room with the dragon but then stopped. "Wait!" he said. "We have to pick a name for her before I go. What do you suggest?"

"How about calling her Dora the Second?" asked the prince.

"Too kingly," said his father.

The queen said, "Since you think she is a gem, let's call her Gemma!"

"Gemma. Excellent!" exclaimed the king.

The king had not left the castle for months. Now he zoomed downstairs, crossed over the moat, and marched into town. His gloomy mood had been replaced by one of joy.

As he approached town, he sensed something strange. The streets were filled with foul-smelling garbage. The cottages were filthy, and the roofs needed repair. Shops were closed. He saw a small number of tired, hungry-looking people on the streets. The king's excitement dimmed.

All the plantings in the town square were damaged or overgrown. The square should have been crowded with people on a Sunday afternoon, but it was empty. No music. No children. No laughter.

King James was shocked by what he saw. How had his kingdom been reduced to this unhappy place? He had only himself to blame. Wellington had fallen on hard times because he had neglected his duty.

He began to pace. "It is time I accepted the fact that Dora is gone and that Wellington needs its king. Things will change. I will repair the damage I have done."

♛ ♛ ♛

The king ran back to the castle to tell the queen what he had decided. She was overjoyed to see her husband behaving like his old self. Once again, he had the twinkle in his eyes that had been missing since Dora disappeared.

Right away, the king started making plans and giving orders. "Anna, I am a changed man. No more brooding. We have a lot to do, but we will get it done if everyone lends a hand."

He sent carpenters and gardeners to repair or replace everything that was damaged. He sent knights and equipment to help every village and farm in the kingdom. Shops reopened and flowers were replanted. Streets were cleaned and repaved with the finest cobblestones. No more muddy ruts.

There was no shortage of helping hands. Everyone pitched in, even the king and queen. Little by little, the kingdom was restored. Life was good again—all thanks to a little dragon named Gemma.

There was only one problem. It was King James who had trained Dora when she first came to live at the castle. Now that the king was managing the repair of Wellington, someone else needed to train Gemma.

Prince Henry wanted to train the dragon. He wanted to please his father and show him that he could handle such an important job. "Father," begged the prince, "may I please be in charge of Gemma's training? I know how to train a dragon. I saw how you trained Dora. I will teach Gemma to behave before you know it."

King James thought about his son's request. The king was not sure that Henry could do the job, but he decided to give him a chance. "Very well, my son. You may take on the task of training the dragon."

Henry was excited! He could not wait to tell Molly about the important task his father had given him.

Sadly, the prince was not a skillful trainer. He found Gemma impossible to control. She simply would not behave. Sometimes she ran away from him. He chased her. Sometimes he could not get her going. He shouted at her. The little gem was turning out to be a big handful!

# How to Train a Dragon

Gemma was difficult to handle. She ran around the castle nibbling on everything she found on the floor—stockings, slippers, boots. She damaged rare and priceless objects when she wagged her gigantic tail.

She loved to plunge her snout into the kitchen garbage, sending scraps of food flying. The cook would chase after her in a rage. If anyone left even a smidge of food on a table, Gemma would leap up and grab it. She greeted people by jumping on them and toppling them to the floor. Nothing and no one in the castle was safe.

But what bothered people the most was that Gemma could not manage her fire-breathing. She kept running around the castle setting things on fire by accident. Once, when the prince bent down to put her on a leash, Gemma sneezed and singed the tip of his nose.

The prince had to admit he was not a successful dragon

trainer. The job was much more difficult than he had expected. He remembered how Molly had soothed the injured eagle. She had a gentle way with animals and was quite clever.

He decided to be humble for once and ask Molly for advice. "Come!" he commanded Gemma, but the dragon did not budge. So the prince put a leash on Gemma and led her to the kitchen.

Molly stood on the edge of a small stool humming to herself and mixing something with a large spoon. She was completely focused on what she was doing, so she did not hear the prince and Gemma when they entered. She was startled when the prince said, "Good afternoon."

"Good afternoon, Your Highness. What brings you here? Aren't you supposed to be training Gemma?"

The prince said, "That is why I stopped by. The training is not going very well."

"I know," said Molly. "People are tired of all the damage that Gemma is doing. That's why I am making a treat to help you with her training. Once she has a taste of it, you will be able to handle her."

♛ ♛ ♛

The prince peered into the bowl. It was filled with a smooth and creamy batter, and smelled sweet. He started to dip his finger into the bowl to have a taste.

"Please don't do that! Wait until it is cooked." scolded Molly.

"I just wanted a sample," said the prince. "Even uncooked, it smells excellent! How long have you been mixing the batter?"

"It feels like forever," she said with a smile as she spooned the batter into a pan and popped it into the oven.

The prince said, "Why did you bother making it?"

Molly said, "I did it for you, Your Highness. I did it because you are my

friend, and you have a problem with this dragon. I wanted to help you." The prince thought that was very kind of her.

The prince and Molly leaned against the edge of the table and waited in silence for the treat to cook. However, Gemma could not sit still. The smell of the treat drove her crazy. She fidgeted and yanked on her leash, trying to get loose.

At last, it was time to get the treat from the oven. Molly managed to slice it into little bits. She offered some to the prince. It was amazingly smooth, creamy, and sweet. The prince smiled from ear to ear. "This is great! Magnificent! What do you call it?"

"Fudge," said Molly.

She stooped down and gave Gemma a bit of the fudge. Within seconds, Gemma settled down. Molly said, "Sit, Gemma!" and the dragon did as she was told. "Good girl," she said as she dropped more fudge into Gemma's eager mouth. Gemma wagged her tail. The prince was impressed.

Molly gave all of the fudge she had made to the prince. "Take this fudge. Give Gemma one bit to settle her down and then more when she behaves. Be sure you praise her when she does."

The prince did as Molly suggested. Within days, Gemma had completely changed. She stopped jumping on people and damaging things. Best of all, Prince Henry was able to teach her how to manage her fire-breathing. No more singed carpets and noses!

From then on, Gemma put her fire-breathing power to good use. She heated the king's bath. She lit fires in the fireplaces to heat the castle and kept the fires going in the kitchen ovens. She melted butter, made toast, and roasted meat. The cooks came to adore Gemma and depend on her.

The prince was overjoyed! His parents were proud of his success with Gemma. They told everyone what a skillful dragon trainer Henry was. The prince was so grateful to Molly. He would not have succeeded without her helpful advice—or her magnificent fudge.

# The King's Holiday

All in all, everything was going well in Wellington. King James was a happy man again. His kingdom was thriving. His dragon was behaving. He decided to celebrate by declaring a holiday for the entire kingdom.

"I will invite people from the four corners of my kingdom and beyond. No one will be excluded. I will get the most wonderful singers, acrobats, and jugglers to amuse everyone. I will hire storytellers, and we will have all kinds of food and drinks."

The king summoned a messenger to the Great Hall. "I want you to go to every farm and village in Wellington and announce that the first Monday in October will be declared a holiday. We are going to hold a festival to celebrate that Wellington is well again! The highlight of the festival will be a joust. The best knights will compete for a prize—a golden goblet!"

The messenger bowed, "It will be done, Your Majesty." He understood that he had an important job to do, and he wanted to get started right away. Within weeks, most of the kingdom had been told about the king's announcement and everyone was making plans to attend the festival.

The morning of the festival, the sun cast a golden light over the town. The air was crisp, but not too cool for an outdoor event. Before the roosters crowed, shopkeepers were setting up their booths. People were decorating the wooden stands with banners. Soon, large crowds of people would start to gather.

Molly woke up with the sun. She did not stop to eat or even talk to her mother because she was eager to get to the festival as soon as possible. She was excited! It was the first time she would attend a festival with a joust, and she did not want to miss a thing.

By the time Molly got to the festival, everything was in full swing. She enjoyed all of it—the roar of the crowd, the smell of the food, the colors of the costumes and banners. Most of all, she wanted to hear the music and the legends that the storytellers told. Molly loved the storytellers the best because she was not able to read. However, her mother and grandmother had told her hundreds of fables and legends.

In those days, dear reader, most children had never been to school or even seen a book. Books were rare and expensive.

Just before noon, buglers stood up in the stands and played a tune from their horns announcing the start of the joust. Over one hundred knights were competing. Molly rushed to the jousting track and managed to get a place to stand right across from where Prince Henry was sitting with his parents and Gemma. She waved and shouted to the prince, but he did not see her.

The king had tightly wound Gemma's leash around the leg of his chair and was waving to the crowd. He stood up and welcomed everyone. He showed them the golden goblet so that they could admire it. It was time for the joust to begin!

Two mounted knights stood facing one another at each end of a track. All eyes were on the knights. The king raised his arm and held it in the air. No one made a sound. Suddenly, he dropped his arm and shouted, "Charge!"

The crowd roared! Both knights yelled as their horses raced down the track kicking up mounds of mud. As the knights got close to each other, they began using their lances to try to unseat each other.

The joust went on until the middle of the afternoon. At last, just one knight remained on his horse. The knight approached the stands, dismounted, and bowed to the king and queen. They stood up together and went down to speak with him.

The king handed the golden goblet to the tired knight and praised him for a job well done. The knight proudly accepted the prize and lifted it high for everyone to admire. The crowd cheered wildly.

Suddenly, a strange look passed across the king's face. He stopped smiling. Something was not right. He sensed it. He looked up at the stands to check if the prince was okay, and the prince waved back. The king started to walk back to the stands. Something made him quicken his step.

As he approached his seat, he gasped. The rope holding Gemma was still wound around his chair, but it had been cut. Gemma was nowhere to be seen. "It's impossible! Where is Gemma?" he shouted. A silence fell over the crowd. Gemma was gone!

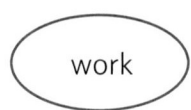

## A Plan is Hatched

Perhaps you find it difficult to understand how it was possible for one king to permit two dragons to disappear. But King James had managed to do it. First Dora and now Gemma. Both gone without a trace.

Everyone was concerned that the king might fall apart again if Gemma was not found soon. Would he neglect their perfect kingdom again? Was everything they had done to repair Wellington going to vanish—just like Gemma? Everyone was in a panic.

This was an emergency! Every person at the festival began hunting for the dragon—in the town, in the woods, and out on the farms. Common people and nobles worked together. Even the king and queen pitched in. They all wanted to be sure that every possible place was checked carefully. They all understood how important it was for the good of the kingdom that they find Gemma quickly.

Molly was concerned. No one had ever found out what exactly had happened to Dora, but this time it was different. It was clear that Gemma had not simply run away or gotten lost because her leash had been cut. What kind of person would steal a dragon?

The afternoon slipped into evening. Molly became more and more concerned. Gemma was gone. No tracks or footprints. With darkness approaching, Molly thought there was no use hunting for Gemma anymore that night. Prince Henry and Molly had agreed to meet after the joust at the castle entrance. "Perhaps the prince is waiting for me," she thought, as she dashed to the castle.

👑 👑 👑

To her delight, Molly saw the prince standing on the bridge next to the gatehouse. He could hear her footsteps as she ran onto the wooden planks. He ran to her and grabbed her arms, his eyes wide with concern. "Tell me! Has Gemma been found?"

Molly sighed, "I'm afraid not."

"This disaster is all because of me. I should have kept an eye on Gemma while my parents were presenting the prize. How could I have let a crook take Gemma from right under my nose?"

"Nonsense," said Molly. "Don't be foolish. Every person at the joust had their eyes on your parents and the winning knight."

The prince said, "I must find her, Molly. I must find Gemma for my father and for Wellington. It is the least I can do. I feel I have let him down. I am only one person, but I will keep looking all night if I must."

"That would be unwise. It isn't safe to go roaming around in the dark. Let me think. Perhaps I can think of another plan."

The prince waited silently. Molly shouted, "I've got it! There is a hermit named Fergus who lives deep in the woods. I visited him once with my grandmother to pick up some powders from him. He is a superb healer and an expert on wildlife."

Molly went on, "Some people say that Fergus can perform magic, but I don't think so. He is just an average person who knows a lot about what goes on in the woods. Let's ask for his advice about how best to find Gemma."

Prince Henry said, "Shall we leave now?"

Molly said, "I don't think so. It's late. Let's get a fresh start in the morning. I will meet you in the kitchen right before sunrise. Together we will bring Gemma home safe and sound. Your father will be so proud of you. You will be a hero!"

"A hero. That sounds perfect! See you in the morning."

"See you," she said and then added, "Your Highness."

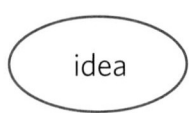

# A Secret Passage

The sun rose while Molly was in the kitchen waiting for Prince Henry. As always, she was a bundle of energy, pacing back and forth. Suddenly, there was a muffled knock at the door and the prince walked in. When she saw his outfit, Molly was startled. He had on another one of his fancy outfits, including riding boots and his crown!

"You're not going to dress like that to trudge in the woods, are you?" she asked and then added, "Your Highness."

"You don't like what I have on?" asked the prince. "I think I look superb."

"Why do you need your crown?"

"How else will anyone we meet know that I am an important person? If I dressed like you, people might think I was a servant."

"I should have known that is what you would say about

your silly crown. But I'm concerned about your safety. Perhaps you might want to get rid of those boots. They look as if they have never been used. The soles are smoother than a frozen pond in winter and twice as slippery."

Molly went on. "You will find it difficult to walk in the woods with them. Your feet will be covered with blisters before we walk a mile. You are a prince. You must own another pair of shoes."

"Nonsense," said Henry. "Don't be a know-it-all. I think I look perfect. Since when did you become an expert on the proper clothing for a prince? Let's get going." He turned to walk to the castle entrance.

Molly mumbled to herself, "So stubborn." Then she called after him, "Wait! If you try to leave by the main entrance, the knights will see you leaving the castle. They are sure to report it to your parents. They will never agree to let you go. I have a better idea. Let's use the servants' passage."

"Servants' passage? There is a servants' passage? I know nothing about it."

Molly said, "It's an old tunnel that starts in the storage room, goes under the moat, and ends outside the castle walls. The servants have used it for years." Molly picked up two candles from the kitchen table. She lit them with smoldering coals in the oven. "Here," she said, handing a candle to the prince. "Follow me."

The prince followed Molly into a huge storage room that was so cluttered that it was difficult to walk. The floor was covered with sacks of flour and huge jars of pickled cabbage. Massive slabs of meat hung from hooks in the beams.

Molly led the prince to a wooden door that was hidden behind stacks of firewood. She pulled the knob and the door creaked open. "Here's the passage. It starts downhill before it levels off under the moat. Then it turns uphill, and we will come out at the edge of the woods."

The prince stepped into the doorway. He had to crouch down so that he did not knock off his crown. All he could see was darkness. The passage seemed to lead into a bottomless pit.

The smells drifting up out of the passage were disgusting—moldy, rotten, nasty smells. Something scampered across his boot. Was it a mouse? A gerbil? A RAT? The prince shivered. He did not know if he was shivering because he was excited or frightened. Maybe a little bit of both.

"Am I supposed to walk down into this black hole?" he asked.

"Yes! That is exactly what you are supposed to do. Just hold onto the wall to keep your balance. Follow me." And with that, Molly disappeared into the darkness.

The prince put his hand on the wall. It felt ice cold and slimy. Everything was wet, as if it had recently rained inside the passage. "What have I gotten myself into?"

He bravely put one foot in front of the other and started down the steep slope, but just as Molly had predicted, his boots could not grip the slippery ground beneath him. He struggled to keep his balance, with no success. Down he crashed onto his knees.

In an instant, Molly was back at his side. "Are you okay, Your Highness?"

"I'm fine," grunted the prince.

"Perhaps I could address you as Your Lowness until you are back on your feet," Molly added with a smile.

He rolled his eyes and stood up. "I slipped and got the wind knocked out of me. I will be better in a moment when I regain my balance." The two friends grasped hands and carefully made their way down the underground passage together. They were still holding hands when they exited into blinding sunlight.

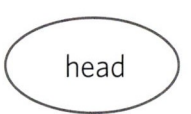

# Good Knight

Prince Henry and Molly managed to get out of the castle undetected. They glanced left and right to check if anyone had spotted them and dashed into the woods. The only sounds in the forest were the chirping of birds and the rumble of a waterfall in the distance.

After a while, the children were getting tired and a little thirsty. They were not making great progress. Their pace was slow because the prince kept tripping on rocks in the dirt. His knees were sore, and he was starting to get blisters on his feet. He hated to admit it, but perhaps Molly had been right about his boots.

It had been foolish of him to choose them. He should have known that the path would be uneven. Still, there was nothing that could be done about the problem now, except to get to Fergus's cottage and give his feet a rest. He asked, "Are we there yet?"

"Almost," Molly said to give him hope, but they really were not close yet. "This is going to be a long day," she mumbled.

They headed deeper into the forest. The sound of the rumbling waterfall got louder and louder. Soon they came to the top of the falls where a wooden footbridge crossed a stream. The water rushed by and cascaded over the edge to the rocks below.

They decided to stop to quench their thirst before crossing the stream. They rinsed their dirty hands and sipped the cool water. Then they leaned against a large birch tree to rest.

They had barely closed their eyes when someone shouted, "You there! Come out! You need a wider tree than that to hide behind. Announce yourselves."

Molly edged from behind the birch tree and stepped in front of a mounted knight. His lance was aimed right at her. "You can tell your friend that he can come out, too!" the knight demanded. The prince adjusted his crown and stepped out from behind the tree. He stood tall, trying to look confident on his blistered feet.

The startled knight scrambled off his horse and bowed. "Your Highness! I had no idea it was you. What are you doing here in the middle of the woods?"

Prince Henry said, "We are on a quest to find Gemma, our dragon. Put down your lance." The knight did as Prince Henry commanded. "Sir, who are you?" asked the prince. "Take off that helmet!"

The knight knelt again and took off the helmet. A tangle of red hair tumbled out. "I am Isabel, at your service." The children were flabbergasted! They had never seen a female knight, and here was a teenage girl dressed in full armor.

"Why are you dressed in armor?" Molly asked.

"It's a sad story," sighed Isabel.

The prince said, "Let's sit down, please. My feet are so sore." They sat on the bridge while Isabel told them her story.

"My father is a blacksmith and a well-known expert in making armor. My twin brother and I have spent our lives at his workshop, playing when we were small and working as we got older. My father always made armor for the two of us on our birthday. We loved to pretend we were knights, fighting battles and jousting."

"Last year, my father had an accident. It has been impossible for him to work for months, so we have fallen behind in our tax bills. We have sold everything we own, except our house."

None of them stirred. Isabel went on, "When the king announced a joust with a fantastic prize, my brother had an idea. He would enter the contest, win the prize, and save the family cottage. However, the day before the joust, my brother fell ill. He was too sick to compete."

"Then I had an idea. I had the armor and the skills needed to replace my brother in the joust, and since I would be completely covered, no one would suspect I was female. My family discussed the plan and thought it just might work."

"Yesterday, I came to the festival and pretended to be my brother. I almost won, but sadly, I came in third. Now, I must go home empty-handed." The three children sat in silence.

The prince thought that was the saddest story he had ever been told. He stood up and turned to Isabel as if he were going to speak. As he did, he slipped on a wet plank and lost his balance. He teetered on the edge of the bridge, windmilling his arms.

Isabel grabbed his arm and dragged him back to safety, but his crown fell into the waterfall. Helpless, they all stared over the edge of the falls. The crown tumbled down, bouncing off rocks as it traveled to the bottom and disappeared.

"My crown," the prince howled.

The girls did not know what to do or say. Finally, Molly spoke up. "Your Highness, what do you want us to do? Your wish is our command."

The prince gazed at the spot where his crown had disappeared, then turned to the girls. He sighed and said,

"I'm afraid there is nothing we can do. My crown is lost forever. I suppose it is time for us to resume our quest."

Isabel mounted her horse, "Farewell to you both, and good luck on your quest."

"Farewell," said Molly. "Good luck to you and your family. I hope our paths cross again."

Prince Henry said nothing. He felt naked without his crown. He was beginning to think that trying to find Gemma might have been a foolish idea.

# Finding Fergus

Prince Henry and Molly trudged on. Their pace was getting slower and slower because the prince was starting to limp. He was sorry he had agreed to hike to Fergus's cottage. The prince was a wreck. His crown was gone, and his feet felt as if they were on fire. He thought they must have been walking all day, but it was still midmorning.

"Maybe we are lost," he said. "You said you had been to Fergus's cottage only once. Are you sure you know where you are going?"

"I am positive. I know exactly where we are. We would have been at the cottage by now if you had not worn those stupid boots!"

The prince said nothing, and they kept walking in silence.

A little later, Molly announced. "We're here!"

The prince looked around and saw nothing but trees and

prickly shrubs. Molly stepped off the path and disappeared between two shrubs. The prince quickly wriggled behind her. No matter which way he turned, there were prickles scratching his hands and catching on his tunic.

They stepped out into a small clearing covered with ferns and moss like a green carpet. A herd of deer was grazing, unbothered by the children's sudden appearance. In the middle of the clearing was a wooden cottage with a family of raccoons asleep beside the door. As the children approached, wrens stopped chirping and poked their heads from nests on the roof.

An old man, bent over with age, his face covered with wrinkles, opened the door when they knocked. His eyes widened with surprise and he broke into a smile. "Molly! So nice to see you."

"Good morning, Fergus. It's great to see you, too." Molly turned and introduced the prince, "This is my friend, Prince Henry."

Fergus looked shocked, but quickly turned and bowed. He said, "Your Highness, welcome to my humble home."

They all headed inside. There was just a single room, with a table and stools, a large cabinet, and a bed tucked in the corner. On the walls, shelves were overflowing with bundles of plants and roots.

"Sit down and rest," said Fergus. "I will fix us some tea, and you can tell me what brings you here."

Fergus saw the prince limp to a stool and sit down. "What's wrong with your feet, Your Highness?"

"Bad shoes," muttered the prince.

"Would you mind if I took a look?" asked Fergus.

The prince winced in pain as he wriggled out of his boots and took off his knitted stockings. His feet were a wreck—covered with sores. Being barefoot felt great.

Fergus asked, "Would you permit me to see if I can help?"

"Please do," said the prince.

Fergus knelt down and carefully inspected the prince's feet. "My goodness! Those blisters look painful."

Fergus hobbled over to the cabinet and opened the doors.

Molly's eyes widened. Books! She had never seen a book before, and she was thrilled. Fergus took out a large book wrapped in cloth. He placed the book on the table and carefully unwrapped it.

Molly asked, "How did you get these books? How many do you own? What does this one say? May I hold it?"

Fergus was amused by her excitement. "You sure can! Just sit down so you don't drop it." He handed Molly the book. She stared at it and then ran her fingers gently over the cover.

"What's the title?" asked the prince.

Molly had no idea what the title was. "I don't know the title. I don't know how to read or write. I never went to school because I had to work with my mother every day."

Prince Henry had never thought about the fact that most children did not go to school. He had had tutors as long as he could remember, so reading and writing were easy for him. More importantly, he wanted to help his friend. "Molly, perhaps I could teach you how to read and write one day?"

"Would you do that? That would be wonderful! Thank you, Your Highness."

"Call me Henry," said the prince.

Molly did not know what flabbergasted her more, the prince's offer to teach her to read or his permitting her to call him Henry.

# In Someone Else's Shoes

Molly handed the book back to Fergus as carefully as if it were made of glass. Fergus said, "The name of this book is *Everything You Want to Know About Wild Plants*. All of my books were gifts from nobles in return for curing their illnesses. Let me see what it suggests for sore feet."

Fergus gently turned the pages until he found the one he needed. Molly looked on in wonder. Each page had been carefully written by hand and decorated with tiny paintings of plants and animals.

Then Fergus gathered some plants and mashed them into a paste. He knelt before Henry and gently covered his feet with the soothing paste that cooled the sores. Then he wrapped them loosely in bandages. Henry's feet stopped hurting him at once.

"Thank you," said Henry with a smile. "I was afraid

Molly was going to have to give me a piggyback ride to the castle." Molly and Fergus burst out laughing.

Fergus said, "Since you took off your boots, your feet have swelled. Unless I am wrong, your boots will hurt you if you put them on again." Now, that was a big problem. How could they go on if Henry were barefoot?

Henry perked up. "I have an idea! Why don't you and I exchange shoes? Our feet are about the same size and your cloth shoes are softer than my boots."

Fergus thought Henry's plan was perfect! They both put on each other's shoes and stood up. Fergus had never owned boots—let alone a pair that belonged to a prince. Henry was happy he could wriggle his feet into Fergus's soft shoes. Problem solved!

Fergus said, "You haven't told me why you are here today."

Henry explained, "Yesterday, our dragon disappeared. Molly thought you might be able to help us find her."

"A dragon? Strange that you should ask. This morning while I was gathering mushrooms, I came across these." Fergus reached into his pocket and opened his fist.

"Dragon scales!" exclaimed Henry and Molly. The scales were dirty, and the edges were curled. Fergus had found proof that a dragon had been in the forest.

Fergus said, "I was surprised to find dragon scales among the mushrooms because dragons hate them. I have found dragon scales deep in the forest from time to time, but never in a patch of mushrooms. A dragon's fire-breathing powers are snuffed out if it eats mushrooms."

"Have you ever seen a dragon in the woods?" Molly asked.

Fergus said, "Only once. Years ago, I met a stranger trudging along with a dragon."

"A stranger? Really?" Henry said, "Do you know where he was going with the dragon?"

"I am sorry. No idea. When I approached him to introduce myself, the man began shouting that I should keep my distance. He was a very unfriendly fellow and wouldn't talk to me."

"Would you please tell us how to get to this mushroom patch?" Henry asked.

Fergus said, "Finding the mushrooms is easy. The difficult part is finding the path. Walk back to the path you were just on and turn left. When you come to the first fork, turn left again. Just as the path curves sharply to the right, you will see a thicket of birch trees.

"Walk to the far side of the thicket. It will be difficult because of the dense undergrowth. Behind the birch trees, you will discover an old path. Keep an eye out for a huge tree stump filled with purple mushrooms. That is where I found the scales. Shall I write it down for you?"

"No, thank you," Molly said. She repeated Fergus's remarks perfectly.

It was time for Henry and Molly to get going. They still had an urgent job to do. Both of them would have loved to stay longer and explore the books and chat with this interesting man. They would have liked to hear how Fergus came to live by himself in the woods. All of that would have to wait for another day.

They all stood outside the cottage and said their farewells. Fergus checked that Molly remembered exactly how to find the mushroom patch. He bowed one last time to Henry, and the children were gone.

# Whistling in the Wind

Hours passed. Henry and Molly trudged on as the path took them deeper and deeper into the woods. The tree limbs were so thick that they blocked out the sunlight. The woods were starting to feel dark and a little frightening. The children had the strange feeling that they were being followed by unknown eyes. Were there ghosts lurking behind those trees?

Molly started whistling. Her tune broke the silence around them.

"Where is that thicket of trees Fergus told us about?" asked Henry. "Shouldn't we have seen it by now?"

"Not really," said Molly. "Before we see the birch trees, the path has to curve to the right." She started whistling another tune.

"Would you please stop that whistling! Honestly, I am sick and tired of listening to it," Henry complained.

"Whistling relaxes me."

"Well, it disturbs me! This is what happens when you go on a quest with a witch."

"Don't call me a witch!" Molly snapped. "Just because I know all about using herbs and how to treat animals doesn't mean I am a witch. If I bother you so much, why don't you just return to your cozy castle? I will find Gemma on my own."

"Who do you think you are talking to? Do I have to remind you that I am your prince?"

"Who do you think you are talking to? Do I have to remind you that I am your friend?"

With that, they stood staring at each other in silence. "I'm sorry," Henry said.

"I'm sorry, too." Molly said.

"Maybe we should walk a little faster." She took Henry's hand and they started walking. The path turned left two more times until, at last, it curved to the right. There it was—a thicket of birch trees! The children ran to it as if it were a long-lost friend.

"What now?" Henry asked.

Molly remembered what Fergus had said. "Fergus told us to walk to the far side of the thicket. Let's do it."

Walking in the thicket turned out to be much more difficult than the children expected. There was no path in the thicket and the undergrowth was dense with vines and prickly shrubs. They had to keep yanking off thorns that got snagged on their clothing. They slowed to a snail's pace as they worked their way between the tightly packed trees. When they reached the end of the thicket, they stopped for a rest.

"Honestly," Molly complained, combing twigs out of her hair with her fingers. "A bird could nest in my hair right now."

But Henry wasn't listening. "Molly! Look!" Just beyond stood the huge stump of a fallen tree. The stump was covered by a large patch of purple mushrooms.

"This is it," said Molly. "This is where Fergus found the dragon scales. What do we do now?"

Henry said, "I'm not sure. Maybe we can find more scales that will tell us which way this dragon went."

"Good idea!" They began combing the ground next to the stump. They walked around the stump in growing circles, looking for scales. As they got farther away from the stump, the ground became soggy, and their shoes stuck in mud.

Soon the excitement faded. Molly sighed, "Honestly, Henry. This is like looking for a needle in a haystack."

"Keep going," he urged her.

It seemed as if they had been looking for hours when Molly shouted, "Quick! I found something! Come look."

Henry ran to her side. What he saw surprised him. Footprints! In fact, two sets of footprints! One set looked like it had been made by a person, but the second set looked as if it had been made by an animal. The footprints seemed to lead away from the path and to the cliffs in the distance.

"Shall we follow them?" he asked. Molly nodded.

After following them for a while, Henry stopped. "Listen! What is that sound?" They both listened. "It sounds like an animal. A very large animal."

Molly put her fingers to her lips and Henry nodded. "Let's not make a sound." They followed the footprints in silence, cringing when their feet made squishy sounds in the mud.

The footprints led them to a row of dense, prickly shrubs. Gently, Henry parted the branches and peered to the other side. A man was asleep on the ground, snoring like a hog. Not far away sat a sad looking dragon. Not just any dragon. It was Gemma!

## A Silent Getaway

Gemma! They had found Gemma! But between Gemma and the children lay the sleeping man. Gemma was behind him fastened to a tree by a rope. "What should we do now?" asked Molly.

Henry whispered, "The first thing we should do is keep our voices down. I don't want the man to awaken. Do you think it is possible for us to free Gemma without making too much noise?"

"Maybe. But what if Gemma gets excited when she sees us and becomes noisy?" whispered Molly.

"I have an idea," said Henry. "Remember how you soothed that injured eagle? Do you think you can do it again? You keep Gemma from making any noise while

I sneak behind that tree and unfasten the rope. Do you think that might work?"

"What if the man is a light sleeper?"

Henry said, "You have a point, but listen to that snoring. From the sound of it, I suspect he is in a deep sleep. I think we can avoid being noisy if we are careful."

"And if you are wrong?" Molly asked.

"What choice do we have? I'm not overjoyed with this plan. But if we go for help, the man and Gemma may be gone by the time we return."

Molly thought about Henry's idea. She could not think of a better one. "Let's do it, but first some advice." She pointed to the tree where Gemma was fastened. "Try to avoid holding on to that tree. It's covered with poison ivy!" Henry gave her a thumbs up.

Molly reached into her pouch and took out her chain. She headed for Gemma, swinging the chain back and forth and whispering softly. Gemma saw her and stood up, as if she were about to run to Molly. But as Molly got closer, Gemma sat back down and just stared at her.

Meanwhile, Henry had reached the tree. He was a bundle of nerves and his hands shook. He unknotted and unwrapped the rope without a sound, carefully avoiding the poison ivy. When Gemma saw Henry, she jumped with joy. He quickly led her back to the underbrush. The sleeping man did not budge.

The children did not have time to stop and enjoy their escape. They wanted to put as much distance between themselves and the dragon-stealer as possible. They were excited and happy that their plan had been successful, and that they were on their way home with the dragon.

Once they had found their way back to the main path, the children turned left to head back to town. Gemma, however, turned right. "Gemma, you are going the wrong way!" Henry said without raising his voice too much. Gemma kept going. "Gemma! Come!" Gemma stopped, turned, and trotted away.

Molly said, "I think she wants us to follow her."

"Follow her where?"

"I have no idea," said Molly. "But I don't think we have a choice. If we let her out of our sight, she just might disappear again."

For an hour, the children followed Gemma. The dragon seemed to know exactly where she was going. It was clear that she was not trying to run away because sometimes she slowed her pace and waited for them to join her.

The dragon turned into a clearing and started running faster. "She's headed to the hills," said Henry, picking up his pace. Gemma was racing ahead, and the children struggled to keep up with her.

At last, Gemma stopped at the bottom of a steep hill. By the time the children reached her, they were panting. Henry gasped, "What now?" Before Molly could speak, Gemma started up the rocky slope and the children quickly followed.

Molly scrambled ahead of Henry. She shouted, "Henry! Look!" as she pointed to the entrance of a large cave.

Henry climbed up over the rocks trying to keep his balance. He refused to look down as he climbed higher and higher. When he reached the cave, Molly was alone. "Where's Gemma? he asked.

"In there," Molly said pointing into the darkness.

They stared into the cave. They could not see a thing. It was as dark as night—even darker. And then a strange noise broke the silence. It was creepy—something between a cry and a moan. It did not sound human.

"I suppose we have to go in and get her," Henry sighed.

"I suppose we do," Molly said as she took Henry's hand. Together they stepped into the mouth of the cave.

# Deep, Dark, and Damp

At first, the children could see nothing because the cave was pitch black. The air was cold and moist. It smelled unpleasant. As their eyes adjusted to the darkness, they saw that the cave was even larger than it looked from the outside.

Water dripped down the walls and seeped into the soil beneath their feet. Bats were flying above their heads. The sound came again, scattering a cloud of bats above their heads. "What was that noise?" asked Henry as he took a deep breath.

They walked to the back of the cave trying to avoid the rubble and animal bones littering the cave floor. And then they saw them. Not one, but two dragons! Gemma was sitting next to an adult dragon! The large dragon seemed sad and unhealthy. She moaned again, and Molly approached to see if she could help.

The sad-looking dragon had a lead ankle cuff that was fastened to the back wall with a chain. She was straining to yank her leg out of the cuff with no success. Instead of freeing herself, the dragon had had only managed to make her ankle sore. Henry approached to lend a hand. That is when he noticed the gold scale on the end of her tail.

At first he was speechless. Then he said, "Dora? You are alive! It is me, Prince Henry!" At the sound of Henry's voice, she yanked at the ankle cuff with even greater force.

The children struggled to help her. They yanked on the heavy chain until they were breathless. They struggled to pull the heavy chain out of the wall. They strained to loosen the lock on the cuff. Nothing worked. At last, Molly suggested that Henry look outside for a strong branch to wedge between the cuff and Dora's ankle.

As Henry rushed back to the entrance, he saw someone approaching the cave. He could tell by the man's clothing that he was the person who had been sleeping near Gemma in the forest. When the man got closer, Henry was able to see his face. It was the peddler, Silvester! Silvester was the dragon-stealer! Henry was full of rage. How dare that man steal the royal dragon!

Henry shouted to Silvester, "Stop!" He had no idea how he could stop Silvester from coming into the cave. Still, it felt like the right thing to say. "I am Prince Henry of Wellington! I command you to stand still." He glared at Silvester coldly. For a moment that seemed to work.

Silvester was so surprised to hear a human voice that he stopped in his tracks. But when he saw Henry, Silvester sneered and took a step closer. "You! What are you doing in my cave?"

"I order you to stop! These dragons are going back to the castle," bellowed Henry.

Silvester chuckled and took another step. "Well, you can keep the large beast. She turned out to be a huge disappointment. I was getting wealthy selling her scales to fools who thought they were good luck. But everything changed after I sold her baby to the queen. The dragon stopped eating. Without eating the bits of mushrooms I hid in her food, her fire-breathing power returned. I haven't been able to get near her since."

Henry was flabbergasted! Dora was Gemma's mother! "These dragons don't belong to you. They are coming home with me," insisted Henry.

Silvester laughed. "Dear boy, I can't let you do that. I want that little dragon to replace her mother." With that, Silvester charged at the prince, but Henry was ready for the attack. He lunged at Silvester's legs with all his might. They both fell to the ground.

Suddenly, there was a deafening roar—so frightening that Henry and Silvester both stopped struggling and jumped up. There was a second roar. And then a third one that shook the ground beneath their feet.

An enraged Dora stood in the entrance of the cave, spreading her wings. She was ready for battle. Her eyes were red with anger. She raised herself up on her hind legs and exhaled her fire breath. Smoke puffed from her nostrils as she glared at Silvester. Dora was a fearsome sight!

That was all Silvester had to see. He turned and ran for his life, screaming at the top of his lungs. Fear gave Silvester a lot of energy, but he could not outrun a dragon. Dora followed behind him, keeping a steady stream of flames aimed at him. Silvester was last seen running out of the kingdom with the seat of his pants on fire!

# Home Sweet Home

Henry watched Dora chase Silvester until they both disappeared from sight. As Henry sat down to catch his breath, Molly and Gemma came running out of the cave. "Are you all right?" Molly asked.

"I'm fine," said Henry.

"What was all the commotion about?" asked Molly. "Where is Dora?"

"Dora is making sure we will never see Silvester again."

"Who is Silvester?"

Henry said, "That's a long story. I will fill you in later. More importantly, may I ask you a question? How did Dora get loose from the chain? Did you use one of your magic potions again?"

"The solution was easy. No magic potions," explained Molly. "Just a small amount of olive oil. I always have some in my pouch because it comes in handy. My fingers were numb from the cold air, but I managed to dribble the oil between the cuff and Dora's leg. It worked like a charm! As soon as we heard you yelling, Dora reared up and with one powerful yank, she won her freedom. A combination of olive oil and anger did the job."

The excitement was over for the moment and the children sat down and waited for Dora to return. Gemma joined the children. She put her head in Molly's lap and her other end in Henry's lap. He did not mind. He scratched her scales with affection. No sooner had Gemma settled down, than she picked her head up and began wagging her tail wildly.

In the distance, they spotted Dora racing back to the cave. When she reached the cave, the dragon was breathless. She had stopped shooting flames, but smoke was still coming out of her nostrils. She nuzzled Gemma and accepted gentle scratches from the children.

"We should get going," said Henry. "It's getting late."

"I'm ready," said Molly.

"Do you know which way we have to go?" asked Henry.

"Sure, we have to go back across the meadow to the path and then reverse Fergus's instructions. I could do it with my eyes closed!"

So, the four of them—two children, two dragons—started back to town. Henry and Molly rode on Dora's back, while Gemma trotted alongside. Molly was thinking about what an astonishing day it had been.

Henry was thinking about what his father would say when he saw both dragons were safe. Their day had been a complete success.

♛　♛　♛

The day began to turn to night and the children were getting drowsy. Suddenly, they were startled by the sound of hoofbeats ahead of them. Henry said, "What now? I've had all the excitement I can take for one day."

They were surprised to see Isabel trotting their way. Isabel was even more surprised to see Henry and Molly riding a full-size dragon! Isabel remarked, "That is strange transportation! And not just one, but two dragons! I see you had a successful quest."

"What are you doing in the middle of the forest at this late hour?" asked Molly.

"As a matter of fact, I was looking for the two of you. I wanted to return this to the prince." Isabel reached behind her and took out Henry's royal crown!

Henry was so astonished. "My crown! Where did you find it?"

Isabel explained, "After we parted, I made my way down to the stream. When I stopped to quench my thirst, I saw something glistening in the water. I have been hunting for you for hours. I know how much this crown means to you." She handed the crown to the prince with a smile.

Henry said, "I think you need that crown more than I do. Selling it will bring you much wealth. Having the crown is a solution to your family's problems."

Isabel's voice was choked with emotion. "Your Highness, that is too great a gift for me to accept."

"Nonsense," said Henry. "My head feels much better without that heavy crown, anyway. Please take it."

Molly was proud to hear her friend's suggestion. "This prince will be a fine king someday," she thought.

"Thank you, Your Highness. I will never forget your kindness," said Isabel with a bow. "Now, I had better get home. It is starting to get dark already. Farewell, my friends."

"Good night, Isabel," said Molly.

"Good night, good knight!" said the prince, and he burst out laughing.

At first, Molly just stared at her friend in shock. His head was bare, his clothing dirty, and his body was sore. Yet he was laughing, not just a smile or a giggle, a real belly laugh. She grinned and then she joined in. The two laughing friends returned home after a long but wonderful day together.

Well, that's the end of my story. I hope you enjoyed it. You may think it is fiction, but it is not. Everything I wrote really happened. I heard the story from my mother, who heard it from her mother. Did I mention that my grandmother was Molly?

King James and Queen Anna were thrilled when everyone returned safely. There was a celebration like no one had ever seen! The celebration lasted for days.

They set up a preserve for dragons—a safe place where any dragon could live with their family. In time, the population in the preserve was over a thousand dragons! Dora and Gemma lived in the castle for the rest of their lives and visited the preserve almost every day.

You might be interested to know that the king gave my grandmother Molly a bag of gold coins for her assistance in saving the dragons. She used the gift to open a shop in town where she prepared and sold herbs and other organic cures. People came from far and wide for her advice and she became quite well-known.

Prince Henry kept his vow to teach my grandmother how to read and write. She, in turn, made sure all her children had a good education. My mother even opened the first public school in Wellington.

Are you wondering what happened to the prince? It's no surprise that Henry became the king of Wellington. He was well-known for his wisdom, his honesty, and his kindness. He was called King Henry the Great.

Molly and Henry remained friends for the rest of their lives.

Edwin

The **PAF Reading Program** provides decodable, controlled text for beginning readers. *Decodable* means the words presented contain only letter sounds that children have been taught, so that they can sound out words. *Controlled* means that there is repetition in the vocabulary, allowing children to begin to recognize common words, with the length of words and sentences increasing gradually.

The Reading Series follows the instructional sequence in *PAF*, but it can be used to supplement any reading program. Each decodable chapter book in the series has a corresponding **Teacher Edition** and **Skills Book** for teaching accurate and fluent reading, comprehension, vocabulary, handwriting, and spelling.

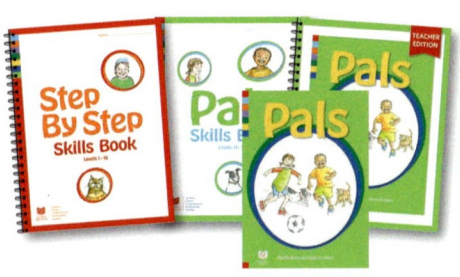

## Pals
- Consonants *b, c, d, f, g, h, j, l, m, n, p, r, s, t, v, y*
- Short vowel *a*
- Suffix *-s*
- Nonphonetic Words *the, to, you, your, said*

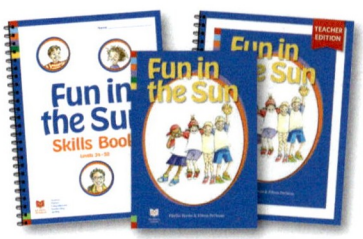

## Fun in the Sun
- Consonants *k, w, x, z, qu*
- Short vowels *i* and *u*
- Nonphonetic Words *of, are, they, put*

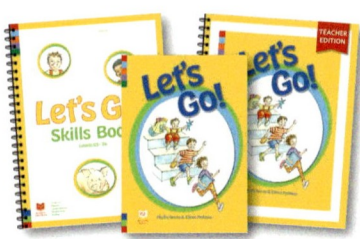

## Let's Go!
- Short vowels *o* and *e*
- Digraphs *ch, sh, th*
- Suffixes *-ing, -ed*
- Compound Words
- Nonphonetic Words *was, from, were, very, do, goes*

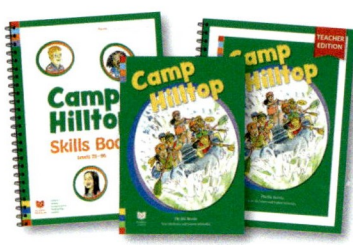

### Camp Hilltop
- Final Blends
- Two-Syllable Root Words: VCCV *(rabbit)*
- Suffixes *-es, er*
- Contractions
- Nonphonetic Words *don't, won't, who, school, want*

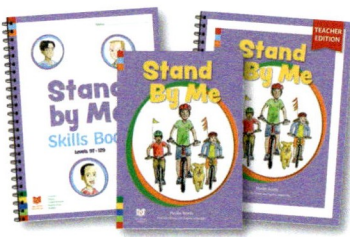

### Stand By Me
- Initial Blends and R-controlled Vowels *-ar* and *-or*
- Two-Syllable Root Words VCV *(robot)*
- Suffixes *-est, -ful, -less*
- Nonphonetic Words *one, done, none, what, there, some, come, off, walk, talk, where, friend, full*

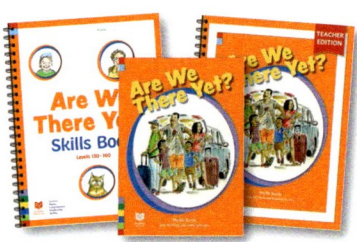

### Are We There Yet?
- Common Long Vowels
- Suffixes *-en, -y, -ly*
- Homonyms
- Nonphonetic Words *could, would, should, their, sure, says, does, only, again*

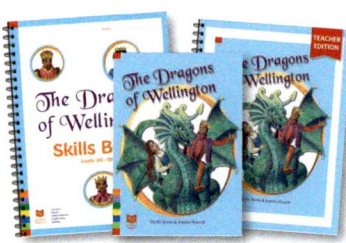

### The Dragons of Wellington
- Multisyllable Root Words *(president)*
- Vowel Digraphs *(oo, oi, ou)*
- Soft *c* and *g*
- Special Syllable Endings *(puzzle)*
- Syllable Division VCCCV *(hundred)*
- Affixes *re-, un-, -ness, -ment, -tion*

PAF is a comprehensive program for teaching reading, writing and spelling in the primary grades using multisensory techniques. For more detailed information about multisensory reading instruction and the specific instructional techniques used in PAF, visit

### pafprogram.com